African American Adult Male Head of Households

Where Are They?

Dr. Jim H. Copeland Jr.

ISBN 978-1-0980-3633-1 (paperback)
ISBN 978-1-0980-3634-8 (digital)

Copyright © 2020 by Dr. Jim H. Copeland Jr.

All rights reserved. No part of this publication may be reproduced, distributed, or transmitted in any form or by any means, including photocopying, recording, or other electronic or mechanical methods without the prior written permission of the publisher. For permission requests, solicit the publisher via the address below.

Christian Faith Publishing, Inc.
832 Park Avenue
Meadville, PA 16335
www.christianfaithpublishing.com

Printed in the United States of America

Contents

Introduction 5
Chapter 1 7
    Background 7
    African American Absenteeism as a Complex
        Social Phenomenon 8
    Media/Social Influences 10
    Other Influences on Absenteeism 12
Chapter 2 15
    Occurrence on Absenteeism in
        African American Families 15
    Peculiarities of African American
        Adult Male Absenteeism 22
    Consequences of African American Adult Male
        Absenteeism 29
Chapter 3 35
    Economic, Social, and Cultural Impact of African
        American Adult Male Absenteeism 35
    Addressing the Problem of Male Absenteeism in
        African American Families 43
Chapter 4 50
    Adult African American Males—From Their Perspective ... 50
    Views on Marriage 51
    Growing Up in a Two-Parent Home or Not 52
    Female Head of Household 53

    The Ability to Change Present Circumstances as
        they Relate to their Children 54
    Relationship with their Children 55
    Relationship with Your Father 56
    Employment 57
    Conclusions 1 57
    Conclusions 2 58
    Conclusions 3 59
References 61
Appendix A: Interview Questions for Selected Participants...........67
Appendix B: Employment..69

Introduction

Parental involvement impacts the emotional, psychological, and spiritual development of children. In 1956, 75 percent of African American homes had an adult male as part of the two-parent household; however, in 2011, 32 percent of African American homes had an adult male as part of the two-parent household. An increasing number of African American adult males are leaving their children behind and abandoning their responsibilities as fathers. Understanding their reasons for leaving is the purpose of this book. In the African American community, all too often the adult male is absent from the parenting role. More research is needed to address the feelings and experiences of African American adult males and their perspectives on the disproportionate decline in male-led households. Interviews were conducted with twenty-six fathers. The research questions addressed the perceptions of African American adult males about the decline in male-led households. Interviews, direct observation, and documentation were used to triangulate the interview responses. Categories and themes were identified as well.

Chapter 1

Research indicates that the African American adult males encounter many challenges to their personal view of themselves. This includes a lack of education (Heckman 2011), underemployment, and unemployment (Ritter and Taylor 2011). Additionally, African American adult males experience a high rate of incarceration, alcoholism, and drug use (Holzer, Offner, and Sorensen 2005; Barton, Kogan, Cho, and Brown 2015). This population present with low self-esteem (Warren-Findlow, Seymour, Brunner, and Larissa 2012) and crime involvement (Lofquist et al. 2012) as well. Many African American adult males had few positive male role models and often endured fatherlessness as well (Heckman 2011; Kogan, Yu, and Brown 2016).

Background

The African American adult male's role as a provider and protector has not changed over the years (Heckman 2011). African American families are facing increasing fatherlessness and a decline in the continuity of the African American home (Hudson, Neighbors, Geronimus, and Jackson 2012). The African American adult male, because of the moral decay within the African American community, has changed his view of himself as the head of the household (Abrams, Maxwell, and Belgrave 2017). Social media coupled with poor role models have left African American adult males with little guidance or direction and poor self-esteem (Father's Rights 2013; Kogan et al. 2016). Often, young African American males are identifying their manhood through their procreation outside of marriage. These actions result in the continued and increasing rise in young unwed mothers and teenage pregnancies (Kogan et al. 2016). This perception of themselves, women, and the family unit adds to society's poor social viewpoint of African American adult males. Continued maladaptive behaviors often lead to criminal activity as well (Barton et al. 2015). Research concludes that one in four African American males are incarcerated, and this number is increasing (Barton et al. 2015). Additionally, the national divorce rate for all ethnic groups remains at around 47 percent in the United States while the divorce rate for African Americans is 50 percent. The divorce rate for African American families is indicative of the breakdown of the family unit (Heckman 2011).

There has been an increase in African American adult males who are interested in maintaining contact with their children, therefore assuming their role as fathers (Kogan et al. 2016). This is in part due to the encouragement of the biological mothers, family members, and the legal system. Unfortunately, this increase in interest is limited to visits on some weekends or during the summer months (Adkison-Johnson, Terpstra, Burgos, and Payne 2016). Those fathers who have an interest in parenting (Richardson and Van Brakle 2013) and nurturing their children often do not state the true reason for their initial separation or departure from their offspring (Varga and Gee 2017).

African American Absenteeism as a Complex Social Phenomenon

In-depth understanding of absenteeism in the context of family relations seems impossible without presenting a brief insight into absenteeism as a general concept. Overall, since the nineteenth century, the term absenteeism has been traditionally treated as an indicator of poor individual performance (Unger 2007, p. 110). Absenteeism is a failure to appear at work or inability to perform another regular duty owing to one's own absence. In organizational terms, absenteeism is a management problem reflecting a breach of an implicit contract between employees and their employers (Unger 2007).

It is reasonable to admit that absenteeism is frequently viewed as a negative phenomenon reflecting a failure in a certain organization. As Bianchi, Casper, and King (2005) implied, absenteeism can be understood not only as an employee's non-presence at the workplace, but also as a physical or financial absence of a family member within a family structure. According to Greene (2011), each family should be treated as an organization or a structure in which the presence of all components is essential. Bellamy, Thullen and Hans (2015) added that if a family is treated as a social organization with its own homeostasis, absenteeism reflects a failure or imbalance in an organizational structure.

The topic-related literature suggests that the so-called presenteeism is significant for well-being of a family as a social organization. Donnellan and Jack (2009) defined presenteeism as a phenomenon opposite to absenteeism or a positive concept reflecting one's presence at a given setting for performing corresponding duties (p. 114). Doyle, Pecukonis and Lindsey (2015) revealed that a family can be viewed as a social organization in which each parent has his or her social roles and responsibilities. These responsibilities are difficult to replace by another family member. In the context of a traditional family, a father's role is usually assumed by a male who assumes the position as a family head, while a mother's role belongs to a person who performs the functions of manager-treasurer of the household. The eldest of the children may assume the parental role only in the case when a father or a mother is away from home (Richardson and Van Brakle 2013). Besides, both parents are supposed to take care of their children, to take part in their education, to ensure their good health, etc. (Williams, Banerjee, Lozada-Smith, Lambouths, and Rowley 2017). Presence of both mother and father in a family structure is paramount for the normal family functioning.

However, the significance of male members for a family is determined not only by a patriarchal culture, but also by Attachment Theory. According to Varga and Gee (2017), focusing on the effects of early bonding between children and their caregivers, this theory implies that emotional attachment to a father plays a significant role in offspring's normal individual development. According to Threlfall and Kohl (2015), a parent-child interaction is vital, since it provides children with essential behavioral models to be copied in adult life, influences the formation of significant traits of character and plays an indispensable educational role, etc. Correspondingly, the absence of a child's emotional attachment is likely to make children's development abnormal (Richardson and Van Brakle 2013). Overall, based on the information presented above, one may agree that in the context of family relations, male absenteeism is characterized as a negative rather than positive phenomenon.

It is essential to mention that absenteeism of a male family member is usually associated with a fatherless family (sometimes called as an incomplete or single mother family). The literature implies that being a complex social phenomenon, father absenteeism among African American families becomes problematic which is determined by external influences (Doyle et al. 2015). It is reasonable to mention that even in the early years of the New World development, respect for a father as the key and indispensable family member was evident in the African American community (Richardson and Van Brakle 2013). As Bellamy et al. (2015) reported, at that time, enslaved black children displayed loyalty to their father for resisting the effort of white slave-owners to break their family relations. At the same time, the institution of slavery had a negative impact on the consciousness of the black male, since black men usually became primary victims of their white masters' violence that, in its turn, has a damaging effect on black masculinity (Threlfall et al. 2015). Bellamy et al. (2015) argued that although the influence of slavery on black men was malicious and dehumanizing, the fact that the African American father is a resourceful and viable entity in the home remains undeniable.

Media/Social Influences

Media influence also had a negative impact on a father's image in African American families. In the second half of the twentieth century, such television programs as *Good Times* and *The Jefferson* provided the US society with a belief that an African American father is a strong, stern, and frustrated man owing to his disadvantaged status as a black man (Abrams et al. 2017). Although this racial stereotype could reflect reality, it created a stigma of anger and questionable judgment on behalf of black fathers. As a result, black men's distrust and dislike in relation to white US people grew (Meschede, Thomas, Mann, Staff, and Shapiro 2016). In their turn, white people ridiculed an image of a barely-making-ends-meet father thought to be presented in all African American families (Abrams et al. 2017). An image of an African American father was marred by stereotypes of a racially obsessed society that perceived an African American family as a symbol of inequity, social dysfunction, and frustration.

At the same time, nevertheless, media influence had a positive effect on African American fathers' self-perception, since the negative experiences made them stronger, more resilient, and determined in providing for the family in the harshest times (Meschede et al. 2016). It is essential to note that the television series *The Cosby Show* depicted a new socially equitable image of an African American father (Thames et al. 2013). To be more specific, the utopian portrayal of a contemporary black father who worked as a white-collar worker and was funny and affluent (rather than angry and frustrated) was presented (Collins et al. 2015). Overall, one may admit that both historical and cultural circumstances influenced the perception of African American fathers by the US society.

Against the background of the information mentioned above, one may agree that excessive public attention African American families, in general, allowed identifying the problem of male absenteeism before it acquired an epidemic character. Abrams et al. (2017) reported that male absenteeism has become a widely spread phenomenon exactly in African American families, where a child grows solely with a single mother. According to the statistics, 50 percent of African American children live with their single mothers (Abrams et al. 2017). It is reasonable to specify that as Adkison-Johnson et al. (2016) revealed, the likelihood of being grown in single-father families is extremely low in the African American community and can be faced only in 5 percent of cases. According to the statistics, in the USA alone, only "29% of African American children live with their married parents, while the rate for all American children living with their married parents is 61%" (Fathers' Rights 2013, para. 3). Meshede et al. (2016) also noted that seven in ten white children in the USA live with both parents. For comparison, Thames et al. (2013) noted that 72 percent of African American children are born in single-mother families, while these figures for the representatives of other American communities are significantly lower. For example, according to the author, 29 percent of whites, 17 percent of Asians, 53 percent of Hispanics, and 66 percent of Native Americans were born in fatherless families after the year 2008. This way, the problem of absent fathers is believed to be more peculiar for African American families than for those belonging to other communities (Collins and Perry 2015).

Other Influences on Absenteeism

Against the background of statistics provided above, it is not surprising that many African American families are incomplete and usually include a single mother and a child (or children). Bryant, Haynes, Greer-Williams and Hartwig (2014) underlined that in these types of families, fathers are absent for different reasons. First, children may be born out of marriage, so they often live with an unmarried single mother; Hudson et al. (2012) mentioned that the number of such children reaches 70 percent (p. 783). Second, African American incomplete families can be a result of a father's premature death; however, the real life number of children who have lost their fathers is insignificant (Bryant et al. 2014). Finally, a mother of fatherless children may have a divorced status, so their father is alive but lives in another house; as Bryant et al. (2014) revealed, "compared with Caucasians, African Americans are less likely to marry and more likely to have children outside of marriage." However, as Moore et al. 2016) suggested, whatever reason for absent fathers in African American families may be, children lack paternal care, while their mothers have to become the only adult responsible for the functions usually performed by fathers in complete families. This way, both a child and a mother face great difficulty in African American single parent families.

In the context of the African American community, fatherlessness is associated with single mother families. Baker (2014) noted that although a single mother can be strong enough to provide for her children, she realizes that it is indeed an extremely difficult task; this way, fatherlessness can be treated as a burden for all single-mother African American families. As Robinson and Reio (2012) clarified, a single-mother family "consists of a biological mother and her biological children, all living in a household that does not include the biological father" (p. 19). Although a biological father can be alive, children in single-mother families are often labeled as fatherless (Non, Gravlee, and Mulligan 2012). The reality demonstrates that uneducated single-mother African American families are likely to become a low-income social group (Robinson and Reio 2012). The material well-being of these families can be restored only in case of either regular financial support (from the government, mother's relatives, friends, etc.) or a single mother's remarriage (Warren-Findlow et al. 2012). However, these cases are an exclusion rather than a rule, so a strong correlation remains between single-mother families and poverty (Non et al. 2012). This cycle of single-mother families among African Americans warrants change through the reduction or elimination of father absenteeism.

Existing research literature provides an idea that the problem of father absenteeism among African American families should be immediately eliminated. Robinson and Reio (2012) mentioned that against the background of recent progress into a more intellectually developed, economic, and technologically advanced age, fatherlessness recognized as one of dangerous "social ills" should be eradicated, since it remains an embarrassment for the contemporary democratic US society (p. 784). Bryant et al. (2014) implied that African American adult male absenteeism has become an economic burden for the United States. Since many single-mother families currently live in poverty; the author clarified that the rate of African American poverty has reached 26 percent, and that exactly fatherless low-income families contribute to poverty development and persistence (para. 11). African American adult male absenteeism presents an urgent social problem that should be solved to insure the overall progress of the United States.

In the twenty-first century, the problem of African American father absenteeism is believed to be urgent owing to its epidemic character. Today's statistics implies that most African American children have absentee fathers; Baker (2014) revealed that the number of such children reaches over 80 percent (p. 783). According to Krogan et al. (2016), special attention is currently paid especially to nonresidential fathers (sometimes referred to as absentee fathers) or those who do not live in the home with their children (p. 282). Taking into consideration that African American men are usually blamed for the rise of the US juvenile crime, increases in single-parented homes headed by black women is expected. High rates of born illegitimate children and rising problem of father absenteeism especially in this ethnic community comes under much scrutiny. Robinson and Reio (2012) provided the idea that since a complete family has been a culturally and socially significant component of the US society, the problem of African American father absenteeism should be solved as soon as possible. However, as Moore et al. (2016) mentioned, the solution of the discussed social problem is impossible without a thorough understanding of all details associated with it.

Chapter 2

Occurrence on Absenteeism in African American Families

To understand why exactly fatherlessness in the African American community has occurred is much more difficult than it may seem. According to Armah (2015), the existence of this phenomenon may often be explained by imperfect individualities and immoral behaviors of African American adult males themselves. The authors provided the idea that black men have usually been characterized as those seeking sexual relationships with women and then pushing them away from meaningful family responsibilities; as a result, a high percentage of young unmarried women (mainly, twenty to twenty-five years of age) with at least one child is peculiar for African American community (Baker 2014). However, the phenomenon of epidemic fatherlessness that has been experienced by African American families for a long time has occurred owing to a complex of reasons, rather than to solely individual factors. In addition, as Franks (Kogan et al. 2013) revealed, the US society still has a distorted perception of African American absentee fathers as "sexual predators, seeking personal gratification and likely to abandon the child and the child's mother when a better opportunity comes along" (p. 788). Against the background of this evidence, the necessity to reveal factors leading to the development of the mentioned problem obviously grows.

African American father absenteeism is a complex social phenomenon the occurrence of which is partly determined by historic circumstances. According to Kogan et al. (2016), in the early twentieth century, African American fathers moved to cities searching for a better job or joining the army during World War I. The author also reported that "families significantly disintegrated under the pressures of city life" (p. 8). Kogan (2016) underlined that African American families have always tended to be stronger in rural communities, so the incidents of family separation have always been more peculiar for urban African Americans. This way, it is not surprising that as Robinson and Reio (2012) report, at the beginning of the twentieth century, rapid urbanization experienced by the rural African Americans favored the destructiveness of their family union. That time, many African American fathers from rural regions arrived at cities "in search of American Dream" hoping to find decent employment in order to provide for their poor families and to ensure their better quality of life (Williams, Mance, Caldwell, and Antonucci 2012).

Another reason for African American adult male absenteeism related to historical circumstances is World War II. In comparison with the previous world war, this one not only greatly impacted the American society in general but also brought negative changes in an African American family institution (Robinson and Reio 2012). As Robinson and Reio (2012) reported, World War II involved over fourteen million men and women (including African American ones) into the armed forces and added another ten million to the labor force (p.19). The war made the US army draft not only single men but also fathers. This way, it was not surprising that World War II led to the separation of husbands from their wives and children. As Baker (2014) underlined, at that time, African American men spent many hours away from their families. According to William et al. (2012), the adverse effects of the war on African American families were evident, since some fathers were killed in combat, while others returned home frustrated or severely damaged. However, as Baker (2014) mentioned, "angry men [are] never able to readjust to family life" (p. 20).

World War II resulted in not only African American men's deaths and frustration but also to mass migration of their families. In addition, numerous African Americans migrated northward during the 1940s. As a result, by the end of the post-war decade, the proportion of blacks in urban areas had exceeded those in rural areas (Robinson and Reio 2012). As Baker (2014) noticed, correspondingly, life in new places made African American families encounter numerous obstacles, including a lack of housing, racism-provoking resistance between white and black communities, discrimination at all levels, and poverty. Kogan et al. (2014) revealed that the life of migrated African Americans was associated with economic hardships. In the middle of the twentieth century, job opportunities were still scarce for African American men. The jobs available were limited mostly to low-paying ones and included manual labor positions, such as hotel clerk positions, stocking jobs in markets, nanny jobs, house cleaning, etc. (Kogan, 2016). As a result, "the mother was often left with the children while the father was left to struggle to make a living" (Williams et al. 2012, p. 22). Overall, the tendencies mentioned above led to black marriage disintegration, out of wedlock birth proliferation, reliance on welfare which, in their turn, influenced the occurrence of father absenteeism (Abrams et al. 2017).

Although African American fatherlessness could be noticed long ago, it has become a real life, serious social problem since the middle of the twentieth century. As William et al. (2012) revealed, since that time, African Americans gained civil rights and better employment opportunities, but their family institution indeed deteriorated. Robinson and Reio (2012) revealed that fatherlessness in the African American community has been evident especially since the post-war years in the USA, when this ethnical group faced severe poverty. According to the author, African American men were then mostly registered as unemployed and roaming drug addicts and criminals unable to either create their own families or provide their existing ones with decent living conditions (Kogan et al. 2016). It is reasonable to admit that the numbers of imprisoned male criminals among the US black citizens were extremely high, so single-mother parenting among African American families became widely spread at that time. In addition, Kogan (2013) revealed that a high proportion of African American fathers were involved in the Vietnam war; many of them did not return to their homes and families. This way, in the 1970s, "an epidemic of fatherlessness" became a widely spread phenomenon among African American US community (Baker 2014, p. 29). Because fatherless children could be faced frequently, by the end of the twentieth century, single mother African American families had not been considered rarity.

Research literature implies that the development of African American absenteeism has been culturally determined as well. Baker (2014) report that this problem appeared before the 1960s. The authors suggested that at the beginning of the twentieth century, African Americans were considered the most impoverished social group living in the US society (Kogan 2014). Correspondingly, these unfavorable circumstances changed African Americans' perceptions of a family institution; therefore, casual sexual relationships leading to non-marital births became an inseparable part of the black culture. Non et al. (2012) explained that the first half of the twentieth century was characterized by economic despair that, in its turn, gave rise to the so-called "culture of despair" (p. 2). As the authors revealed, "young women with limited opportunities to advance socially and economically—either through human capital investments or the marriage market—were relatively more likely to choose early non-marital childbearing, as compared to other women" (p. 3). Decreased quality of life owing to poverty and a low social status breeds a sense of despair that greatly contributes to early non-marital childbearing.

In addition to the mentioned circumstances in which African American father absenteeism developed, one more cultural factor can be traced in the corresponding literature. Hudson et al. (2012) reported that African Americans have usually been considered to have a limited educational level (leading to unemployment) owing to their families' disadvantaged financial status, so marriages in this ethnic community have not been as frequent as they are among the US white population. Overall, poor educational opportunities and a lack of employment create the cultural environment that makes

African American men assimilate negative attitudes and racist sentiments about themselves (Warren et al. 2012).

A gender conflict is frequently seen as one of the main factors triggering the occurrence of male absenteeism especially in the twentieth-century African American community. Baker (2014) revealed that high levels of gender conflicts have assumed an endemic character in the African American culture. The authors specified that a tendency to gender conflicts in his ethnic community is the heritage of slavery (Kogan et al. 2016). As Robinson and Reio (2012) specified, in the period of slavery, family members were brought and sold without regard for family structure; this way, slavery contributed to "a multigenerational legacy of family instability" (p. 342). Robinson and Reio (2012) added that in the second half of the twentieth century, African American gender conflict was aggravated by the fact that black men's economic position was deteriorating, while black women's position was improving (owing to African American social movement that provided women with civil rights). An African American gender conflict is rooted in socioeconomic changes experienced by men and women in the twentieth century.

It is necessary to mention that in the twenty-first century, African American male absenteeism assumed a voluntary character. Williams et al. (2012) reports that the twentieth century characterized by wars and tendencies (migration, poverty, etc.) triggered by them, father absenteeism in African American community was mostly an involuntary phenomenon. However, against the background of the twenty-first century that seems to provide African Americans with equal opportunities, the problem of fatherlessness in this ethnic community seems to be voluntary (Williams et al. 2012).

Some reasons for voluntary African American father absenteeism at the beginning of the twenty-first century can be identified in the existing literature. According to Baker (2014), such structural economic forces as deindustrialization and globalization have significantly decreased the number of high-paying manufacturing jobs; as a result, they were replaced by lower-paying types of employment. Naturally, this phenomenon leads to unemployment and low self-esteem among the African American population. Taking into consideration these economic circumstances, it is not surprising that fatherhood and marriage can be perceived as a great burden those African American men were considered unsuitable to assume (Kogan et al. 2013).

In the literature on African American adult male absenteeism, divorce is characterized as one of the main culprits of today's fatherlessness. As Robinson and Reio (2012) revealed, the reality demonstrates that many African American children have absentee fathers because their parents have divorced. As the author mentioned, "approximately two in three divorces are initiated not by the husbands but by the wives, and the children remaining living with their mothers in 93% of these cases" (p. 685). According to Amato (n.d.), African Americans usually report lower levels of relationship quality, so in contrast to the US Caucasian families, they are more likely to end their marriages in divorce. The prevalence of African American divorced couples with children may be explained by socioeconomic factors (for example, African Americans usually have a lower education level and income) and other reasons (such as personal childhood experience of being brought up in an incomplete family, frequent marital disagreements, etc.) (Hudson et al. 2012).

The literature implies that the pervasiveness of divorce is tightly related to fewer marriages that, in its turn, may also contribute to the occurrence of fatherlessness. Meschede et al. (2016) suggested that the twenty-first century is characterized by the decline of a marriage institution in the US society, in general, and in African American community. Today's decline of marriage is expressed by the fact that a woman voluntarily chooses to be single if she notes that her partner does not have a potential to provide for a family; by the same token, a man avoids marriage if he realizes that he cannot contribute to a woman's economic well-being (Meschede et al. 2012). In case of the African American community, the decline of marriage is associated with the increase of single motherhood. This way, today's African American single-parent families are mostly presented by those in which a child is reared by a single mother (usually young, unmarried, and without a college degree) who serves as the only breadwinner (Bryant et al. 2014).

Besides a divorce and a general decline of the marriage institution, other key reasons for the occurrence of present-day fatherlessness in African American community can be traced in the corresponding literature as well. Hudson et al. (2012) revealed that media influence on the occurrence of the mentioned problem is obvious, since media sources tend to portray fathers as useless figures in the parenting process. As Williams et al. (2012) implied, myths about fathers and their identities limited solely to "sperm donors" created in the media distort traditional values about the significance of a complete family and make people believe in irrelevancy of fatherhood in the African American community (p. 114). It is not surprising that this ideology imposed by media culture breeds African American men's irresponsibility and negative perceptions of a marriage and the family institution in general (Kogan et al. 2013).

Another factor favoring the occurrence of African American father absenteeism is work. Strong (2012) revealed that career demands often become a cause of fatherlessness because working fathers tend to spend many hours at the workplace, away from their children. According to Strong (2012), these working fathers can be work-addicted; this way, their job, rather than their family, becomes their main priority. Strong (2012) reports that work addiction among African American men is as widely spread phenomenon as it is among white US citizens. Employment separates fathers from their families, so it is not surprising that work may ultimately lead to father absenteeism in the African American community.

Incarceration can also be considered a significant factor contributing to the occurrence of African American adult male absenteeism. The statistics demonstrates that there are 34 percent of sentenced African American adult male inmates per one thousand African American adult males; moreover, twenty-eight of African American men are likely to enter a prison over the course of a lifetime (Baker 2014). Robinson and Reio (2012) revealed that present-day US incarceration policies can be considered racist, since excessive attention to exactly African American adult male criminals is paid by the state police officers. As a result, sentencing African American adult males to prison is often associated with single mother households and children's fatherless status (Moore et al. 2016). Strong (2012) noticed that being incarcerated makes it impossible to be a father. However, even if African American fathers are released from prison, they face other difficulties (for example, difficulty of finding employment) that may influence the return of a fatherless status to their children (Strong 2012).

Research also implies that numerous additional factors (that may interact with one another simultaneously) may trigger the occurrence of African American fatherlessness. According to Bryant et al. (2014), employment issues, dysfunctional relationships with a child's mother, absence of marital commitment to marriage, life frustration, selfishness, and personal experience of being grown without a father are only some of them. Kogan et al. (2016) added that these additional factors may lead to father's voluntary abandonment even in case of African American families that may seem happy at the first sight.

Peculiarities of African American Adult Male Absenteeism

In the literature about father absenteeism in African American families, numerous peculiarities associated with this phenomenon can be found. For example, in contrast to many traditional white families, African American ones are not patriarchal in the division of family responsibilities between a mother and a father. Richardson and Van Brakle (2013) mentioned that in most of modern middle class African American families, both sexes are treated equally, and the sense of personal uniqueness is usually fostered since the childhood. Both girls and boys are encouraged to complete their education, to find a proper job, and to accept family duties. Moreover, for African American families, such traits as nurturing and assertiveness are desirable for all individuals regardless of sex (Barton et al. 2015). Richardson and Van Brakle (2013) added that "such nonbiased sex roles and traits are directly related to young African Americans' ability to relate to their future spouse in an egalitarian fashion and to prepare them for flexibility in performing various family roles" (p. 230).

This way, in an African American family model, a mother may perform maternal and paternal family functions. From the perspective of African American families, male absenteeism may not be treated as an intolerable burden, since children's mothers seem to be powerful enough to grow up their offspring without a father's help (Barton et al. 2015).

The literature also suggests that living in a fatherless family, both a mother and a child must bear social and moral stigma. For example, as Stanik, Riina, and McHale (2013) reported, after World War II and the Vietnam War, fatherless military African American families were treated as socially deviant, and financial support of such families was treated by the US government and society as a major burden. It was not surprising that children grown in these families, as well as their mothers, experienced a sense of painful inferiority in relation to white intact families (Stanik et al. 2013). However, even in the twenty-first century, fatherless children (especially those born outside of marriage) and single mothers may also become the subject of social discrimination in their daily life. According to Timme and Lunkenheimer (2015), a single unmarried mother may often be blamed for possessing immoral behavior and having a non-marital child; in its turn, this social disapproval may reduce her further marriage prospects and ensure her unhappy life without social support. Taylor, Mouzon, Nguyen, and Chatters (2016) revealed that in a modern society, a fatherless child can be labeled as "bastard" or referred to as an uncontrolled youngster with criminogenic behavior (p. 158). As a result, mothers and children in African American fatherless families internalize feelings of guilt and shame and become the subjects of social exclusion.

It is reasonable to admit that since many factors prevent African American adult males from becoming good fathers for their children in real life, the problem of male absenteeism goes on existing in the present-day US society. Barton et al. (2015) revealed that low income, unemployment, drug use, criminal activity, and conflicts with their child's mother make fathers staying in contact with his offspring an extremely challenging task. Stanik et al. (2013) added that such additional factors as insufficient education and childcare-related experience may also influence poor fatherhood in case of African American men. Correspondingly, these factors lead to father absenteeism in African American families. Some information about African American fathers leaving their families can be found in the corresponding literature. For example, Barton et al. (2015) reported that most young African American fathers leave their children immediately after revealing their mother's pregnancy. As the author specified, only 20 percent of fathers live with their children five years after their birth (Richardson and Van Brakle 2013, p. 786). African American adult male absenteeism is the product of the complex interaction of different factors that create unfavorable environment for fatherhood.

It is necessary to admit that according to some studies, a father's absence may not necessarily be associated with bad outcomes for children's development. For example, examining children raised in single mother families, Timpe and Lunkenheimer (2015) revealed that "being without a resident father from infancy does not seem to have negative consequences for children" (p. 1407). According to the authors, most mothers were characterized by affectionate and caring behavior in relation to their children and emotional involvement in their offspring's lives; these features alone create a favorable environment for a child's normal socioemotional development (Taylor et al. 2016). In this context, even without a father, a child may be provided with everything needed for normal development. Stanik et al. (2013) added that sometimes, a father's physical presence is even dangerous for children, especially if he is a drug or alcohol addicted or display aggressive and violent behavior. The author concluded that in some cases, an absentee father is better than a father whose presence may harm a child's psyche or traumatize offspring emotionally (Timpe and Lunkenheimer 2015). Absence of father may not necessarily guarantee child abnormal development, while physical presence of father in children's lives may sometimes be even undesirable. As Taylor et al. (2016) reported, parental love is what all children indeed need; in the absence of a father, this love can be effectively provided by a mother alone. Overall, fatherhood can be treated a merely social role that others can play (mothers, stepfathers, mother's relatives, etc.) as well (Barton et al. 2015).

At the same time, the literature implies that single-mother family with an absentee father remains a non-preferred family model for African American community. Taylor et al. (2016) revealed that according to real-life African American fatherless families' experiences, having an absentee and uninvolved father means living a life full of difficulties. The representatives of the Black and Married with Kids (BMWK) staff imply that for African American community, a father's role is not limited to having a biological connection with children, providing them financially, or being physically present in the home (Taylor et al. 2016). For this reason, a nuclear family (consisting of a biological mother and father, and child/children) is treated as a highly essential social institution that may ever exist (Taylor et al. 2016). For African Americans, fatherhood means gaining acceptance and recognition in one's own family, making lifelong friendship relations, being "hero" and living a happy life in general (BMWK staff, 2013, para. 10). In this context, father absenteeism should be treated as a tragedy from African American perspective. It is not surprising that as Richardson and Van Brakle (2013) noticed, "the current generation of children and youth may be the first in our nation's history to be less well-off—psychologically, socially, economically, and morally" (p. 33). Overall, although male absenteeism is considered a characteristic feature of African American families, this negative phenomenon is not embedded in this US ethnic community.

The literature about peculiarities of African American adult male absenteeism provides the idea that this problem is exacerbated by the absence of fathers' contact with their own children. According to Timpe and Lunkenheimer (2015), after a divorce, the most common reason given for fathers not having more contact with their children is the mothers' reluctance to let them maintain the relationships with the offspring. As Barton et al. (2015) underlined, in theory, divorce does not mean disconnection, but in reality, it often does. Taylor et al. (2016) argued that antagonistic relationship discourages the father's involvement in offspring life. Correspondingly, "the father may see the mother as a gold digger who is out to take him down, as a bad mother or as an enemy who is trying to hurt him through the child" (Taylor et al. 2016, p. 37). Moreover, a mother's antagonistic attitude to a child's father leads to the fact that his phone calls are denied, and visitation rights are refused (Taylor et al. 2016). Timpe and Lunkenheimer (2015) revealed that in the USA, family courts follow the stance that "if the mother does not want the child to see the father any more, then that must be what is best for the child" (p. 785). As a result, about 60 percent of African American fathers do not have further meaningful contact with their children after a marital separation (Stanik et al. 2013, p. 787). Being pushed out of their children's lives, they may walk away and exhibit negligence. However, as Barton et al. (2015) noticed, even after a divorce, many of these pushed away fathers have enough knowledge and experience to remain a competent caregiver for their children.

It is reasonable to mention that the level of African American fathers' awareness of what is embedded in good fatherhood is relatively high. Stanik et al. (2013) paid attention that to the 2005-survey question, "What is the most important thing you do for your children?" The answer "provide" was given by most fathers (p. 785). Moreover, for African American fathers, being able to provide and protect is believed to be the main feature of good fatherhood (Stanik et al. 2013). As one may admit, for African American fathers, the issue of basic needs provision is considered the key one in good fatherhood. Against the background of this information, the reason for father absenteeism in African American community seems to be an inability of a male parent to provide for their own children (Richardson and Braklet 2013). Fathers desire to support their children but find it difficult to do so; for this reason, they divorce and live separate lives (Taylor et al. 2016). This evidence reflects that within African American community, absentee fathers agree to leave their family voluntarily because they are aware of their inability to be a good father for their children.

The literature also implies that many absentee fathers suffer from not living with their children. As Stanik et al. (2013) reported, "regarding family and personal relationships, today's African American men are no less sensitive than their forefathers" (p. 786). The reality demonstrates that African American men resort to psychiatrists' services often. Genially seeking for a professional help to release their pain, they come to specialists in family relations. Stanik et al. (2013) noticed that nonresidential African American fathers tend to speak movingly of the meaning of their children in their lives and frequently feel guilty for not having ongoing contact with them. The author also reported that in a psychiatrist's office, they frequently speak about depression, unease, aggravation, shame, fear, anger, and decreased self-esteem mostly associated with ongoing close relations (mainly with a child's mother) in their lives (Timpe and Lunkenheimer 2015). Overall, the information provided above suggests that African American men are unsatisfied with their position of absentee fathers and are evidently frustrated over their absence in offspring's life (Stanik et al. 2013).

Other peculiarities related to the problem of African American adult male absenteeism refer to the level of involvement of fathers in their children's lives. The reality demonstrates that a high percentage of African American children live without any material support of their fathers. Taylor et al. (2016) reported that these fathers (mainly those of young age) are almost uninvolved in their own children's lives financially. Many nonresidential fathers can hardly provide their mother with some money, so they avoid contacts with their mother and prefer not visiting the family they have left (Richardson and Van Brakle 2013). According to the evidence provided by Richardson and Van Brakle (2013), approximately from 50 to 75 percent of fathers regularly pay the full amount of court-ordered support (p.786). As Barton et al. (2015) underlined, this fact reflects the general idea that the US minority group fathers of children outside of marriage are less likely to pay child support in comparison with their white counterparts. Taylor et al. (2016) added that the absence of material support from nonresidential fathers can be explained by the fact that over 2.5 million of them live in poverty (p. 788). In this context, an African American absentee father does not provide his child with financial support because he is simply unable to do so for financial difficulties, rather than thinks that child support is senseless spending.

Overall, much attention to the active involvement of African American absentee fathers in their children's lives has been paid in the existing literature. Taylor et al. (2016) underlined that it is the quality rather than quantity of time that African American children spend with their fathers. Although these meetings can be rare, they positively contribute to child well-being (Stanik et al. 2013). Taylor et al. (2016) underlined that the absentee fathers actively involved in their children's rearing favor the cognitive development of their offspring. In this case, paternal involvement leads to the formation of such positive characteristics in a child as understanding, social competence, self-control, life skills, and adequate self-esteem. As a result, children of such fathers make academic progress (Taylor et al. 2016). Richardson and Van Brakle (2013) added that "fathers who are involved in their children's schools and academic achievement, regardless of their own educational level, increase the chances that their child will graduate from high school and perhaps go to a vocational school or a college" (p. 790). Correspondingly, children of these fathers are likely to have a successful career resulting in high income and financial stability. The literature demonstrates that the African American fathers who go on participating in their offspring's lives actively ensure children's life success in general (Timpe and Lunkenbeimer 2015).

Overall, the literature suggests that financial and non-financial support of absentee fathers has always been underestimated. Taylor et al. (2016) revealed that according to the recent studies, a status of a nonresidential father does not forecast his inability to provide his child with material and emotional support. As the author mentioned, many absentee fathers especially make non-financial contributions to their children, and therefore, remain involved in the life of the family they have left. Toys, milk, diapers, and baby clothes are only some of their non-cash provisions (Richardson and Van Brakle 2013). Stanik et al. (2013) implied that this physical support ultimately has greater significance and permanence than cash payments that may quickly vanish as bills are paid or be even misused. Against the background of the information presented above, one may agree that it is more reasonable for the US society to assist African American fathers' presence in their children's lives, rather than to denigrate them for their absence.

Consequences of African American Adult Male Absenteeism

All complex phenomena have their own consequences, and fatherlessness in African American families is not an exception. The literature provides the idea that one of the evident consequences of this negative phenomenon is a disruption of father-child's contact. Bellamy, Thulen, and Han (2015) revealed that few children see their fathers after their parents' divorce or father's voluntary abandonment. According to this author, "of the children who live with their mothers and a non-resident father, 25% see their fathers less than once a month. 35% of these children never see their fathers at all" (p. 7). However, even if African American children see their absentee fathers, these visits are commonly rare. Correspondingly, the absence of a father-child's contact may negatively influence child well-being in general (Doyle et al. 2015).

The existing literature provides the idea that from a social and child-development perspective, fatherlessness (whether it is determined by a father's death or his voluntary abandonment) has a damaging impact on a child. Focusing on the outcomes of father's voluntary abandonment for African American children, Jefferson, Watkins and Mitchell (2016) reported that a child is likely to cope with a parental death rather than with voluntary abandonment. The author's rationale for this tendency is as follows:

- After a father's death, a child grieves, feels pain, and comes to understand that death is final.
- A father's voluntary abandonment creates "a plethora of psychological ramifications" for the child expressed in anxiety, resentment, self-blame, etc.
- If a father dies, the image of experienced fatherhood lives on in a child's head and heart; besides, a mother helps to preserve the legacy of fatherhood.
- When a father leaves his family voluntarily, a child extremely suffers; in addition, a child sees that a mother is hurt, so

a child unconsciously diminishes a value of fatherhood in general (Jefferson et al. 2016).

Since the significance of a father in a child's life cannot be underestimated, his absence may lead to undesirable consequences. As Seaton, Neblett, Cole, and Prinstein (2013) reported, a father's active involvement in children's lives through interaction (expressed in a direct contact, play, communication, etc.) is beneficial for their development. The author stressed that fathers are essential, since "they help to teach their children values and lessons in solving the problems they may face, and they do so in a way that differs from what mothers contribute" (Doyle et al. 2015, p. 789). In addition, involved fathers serve as role models in their children's lives that affect how well they relate to others (peers, adults, etc.) in society (Bellamy et al. 2015). Correspondingly, absentee fathers are usually uninvolved, so they create unfavorable conditions for their offspring's development. As a result, their children are likely to be unprepared for an adult life, since they may have poorly developed problem-solving skills, values, and essential behavioral models (Williams et al. 2017). Jefferson et al. (2004) added that since fatherless African American children frequently have problems with psychological and emotional development, it is not surprising that their self-esteem and secure sense of self are damaged.

The effects of African American children growing up without a father have been thoroughly discussed in the corresponding literature. For example, according to Seaton et al. (2016), children from fatherless homes (and those from African American community in particular) are more likely to commit suicide, to run away, to be homeless, to suffer from cognitive disorders, to have problems with anger management, to be drug-addicted, and to become imprisoned. Williams et al. (2017) found out that the close relationship between African American children's fatherless status and the development of psychopathology in them is evident. According to the author, juvenile crime/delinquency, teen drug abuse, and school dropout correlate with fatherlessness greatly (Seaton et al. 2013). Williams et al. (2017) added that in comparison to white fatherless children,

African American ones are more susceptible to demonstrating the signs of deviant, antisocial, and even illegal behavior. Doyle et al. (2015) specified that African American boys are even more at risk to display this type of behavior.

Some information about the influence of fatherlessness on African American female children can be traced in the literature. Bellamy et al. (2015) revealed that African American adolescent daughters abandoned by their fathers are at high risk of experiencing early pregnancy. The statistical data demonstrates that the risk factors for teen pregnancy among African American girls are 45 percent for single mother households (Bellamy et al. 2015, p. 50). Jefferson et al. (2016) explained that a fatherless status produces the feelings of pain, frustration, and disappointments in these girls. Trying to avoid these negative feelings, African American teenagers are more likely to be involved in short-run sexual relationships that allow running away from real-life problems. As a result, these relationships lead not only to blurring the lines between love and sex but also to undesirable early pregnancy. Early pregnancy rarely leads to marriage, so it is not surprising that African American teenagers experiencing pregnancy often remain abandoned by their male partners (Bellamy et al. 2015).

Much attention has been paid to the examination of adolescent behavior in African American fatherless children. Williams et al. (2017) provided the idea that "fatherless black adolescent males are much more likely to live in poverty, drop out of school, and become involved in violent crimes than those who live in a two-parent household" (p. 1). The statistical facts provided above point to the fact that the problem of African American fatherlessness is of large scale which includes 47 percent of single-mother families who live below the poverty level; adolescents growing up in single-mother families at least twice are likely to drop out of a high school; to have a child before age twenty, and to be "idle" (to be out of school and out of work) in comparison to the ones being raised by both parents. Fatherless teenagers (males in particular) are at a high risk to become violent criminals; 70 percent of juveniles in state reform institutions, 60 percent of American rapists, and 72 percent of adolescent murderers are adolescents from single mother families (Schumacher 2008, p. 8).

Family's financial hardships, children's expulsion from schools, and their criminogenic behavior are considered widely spread consequences of African American father absenteeism. Strong (2012) underlined that in case of African American community, persistent poverty is considered the most large-scaled problem attributed to fatherlessness. Father absenteeism is often associated with the loss of the major source of income. It is not surprising that according the statistics, "single female-headed homes are at greater risk of poverty than the rest of the general population" (Strong 2012, p. 46). As Doyle et al. (2015) mentioned, among African American single mothers, the severity of this poverty is greater, since these women remain the subjects of discrimination even in the twenty-first-centry USA. In addition, Strong (2012) paid attention to the fact that being abandoned by a family's breadwinner, African American single mothers (especially the divorced ones) face a double dilemma. On the one hand, "she has to raise the children on substantially-less income than what she had when a husband was present," and on the other hand, 'she loses half of her support network and has to find other avenues to care for the children adequately while she works a job that usually inadequately supports her household" (Strong 2012, p. 46). This way, in African American community, a father's loss is often accompanied by a financial burden of the abandoned family that must survive experiencing severe poverty.

Overall, much attention to African American single mothers as the main family breadwinners is paid in the corresponding literature. McVeigh (2013) underlined that one of the consequences of African American father absenteeism is the increase in "breadwinner moms" (para. 2). The author noted that "working mothers are now the sole breadwinners for 40% of US families." It is reasonable to suggest that African American mothers greatly contribute to this statistic (para. 1). Strong (2012) revealed that being abandoned by husbands, these single mothers work hard for to support their family properly. It is clear that long working hours deprive them of the opportunity to be with children. Correspondingly, this situation leads to the following evidence traced in the majority of African American single parent families: hard working mothers being absent all day long, and children left at home taking care of themselves (Strong 2012).

In this context, according to Strong (2012), it is necessary to mention that pain is one of the outcomes of fatherlessness in African American single mother families. To be more specific, after a father abandons a family, both a mother and a child experience feeling of rejection in their everyday life. Doyle et al. (2015) provided the idea that an absentee father breeds feeling of rejection and insecurities in a single mother and her child; besides, father's abandonment gives rise to feelings of disappointment, emptiness, and hopelessness. Strong (2012) reported that this pain is similar to an injury or an open wound, and being once irritated, it may make an abandoned family member cry and suffer. In its turn, this pain created by a father's loss leads to the development of fallacious hopes, especially in children (Seaton et al. 2013). It is reasonable to underline also that in case of male children, absence of a father creates "the raw, persistent, desperate hunger for dependable male love" or briefly, the so-called father hunger (Strong 2012, p.45). According to the personal experiences of abandoned African American children, many of them realize that their fathers are gone forever, but they still hope that they love them (Strong 2012). In addition, as Strong (2012) underlined, this unresolved pain can create an emotional void in a child's soul; as a result, the offspring starts searching something for filling this void. Against the background of this fact, it is not surprising that trying to fill internal emptiness, children are more likely to display deviant and criminogenic behavior (Seaton et al. 2013).

The literature suggests that emotional impact of fatherlessness on African American children is especially serious in the case of males. According to Williams et al. (2017), the demonstration of deviant behavior is more peculiar for abandoned sons than daughters. For revealing the severity of emotional outcomes of a father's loss for pre-school African American adult male children, Strong (2012) provided the following research results: "Emotional correlates of father absence are more prominent when the absence occurred prior to age 6. Examples include intense anger and lower self-control. Childhood psychopathology included nightmares, bed-wetting, fears, and somatic complaints. Emotional symptoms were found to be markedly more severe in boys than in girls" (p. 44).

African American father absenteeism gives rise to pain occurrence in a single mother and in male children. The corresponding literature suggests that an African American family's fatherlessness status may influence single mother's communication styles as well. Focusing on revealing how single mothers answer their children's question "Where is my daddy?" Jefferson et al. (2016) revealed that two major communication styles chosen by single mothers can be identified (p. 1). The first style is characterized by self-silence and lies while the second one—by acceptance and truth. In the first case, single mothers perceive themselves abandoned and unconsciously preserve the internal feeling of being insulted by an absentee father; this way, they self-silence their thoughts about their child's male parent and may even lie to their children hearing the mentioned question. In the second case, women are reconciled to the fact that a father is absent and accept the idea of his "devastating and decimating abandonment," so they often answer the truth to their children regarding their biological father (Jefferson et al. 2016, p. 1). Bellamy et al. (2015) reported that the child's question about a biological father may cause either negative or normal reaction from a single mother. It is reasonable to admit that the communication strategy based on self-silence and lie is associated with a single mother's angriness, aggressiveness, and nervousness, displaying and bad-mouthing (in relation to child's father), while the second one based on acceptance and truth—with being calm, psycho-emotionally balanced, and sensible (Williams et al. 2017). Overall, taking into consideration the gravity of the consequences of fatherlessness discussed above, one may agree with Strong (2012) that this "ill in the African American family structure" should be addressed as soon as possible (p. 28).

Chapter 3

Economic, Social, and Cultural Impact of African American Adult Male Absenteeism

African American father absenteeism appears to have a significant effect on such areas of life as economy, culture, and society in general. It appears logical considering the essence of the concept itself which presupposes withdrawal from important social practices that contribute to socialization and self-fulfillment of society members. This section discusses the implications that African American father absenteeism is likely to have on varying aspects of lives of the selected social group.

Latunde and Clark-Louque (2016) linked the success of people's social performance to their mental health, stressing the antisocial nature of mental disorder. According to the authors, untreated mental conditions may result in such dangerous developments as substance misuse, antisocial and self-harming behaviors, occupational impairment and issues in family relationships, as well as any kind of interpersonal interactions. They also indicate what they call "indirect costs," mentioning such manifestations as premature death, lost productivity, quality of life issues, pain and suffering, expenses for families, as well as absenteeism (Latunde and Clark-Louque 2016, p. 31). The issues mentioned above, including absenteeism, are likely to affect not only individuals, but entail direct consequences for the national rates of economic growth and poverty reduction, as they foster "individual productivity and social cohesiveness" (Latunde and Clark-Louque 2016, p. 31).

Absenteeism at work as contrasted with family absenteeism is one of major socially important manifestations that results in lost productivity linked to excessive costs and expenses for both employers and employees. According to Hudson et al. (2012), "staff turnover, absenteeism, and performance levels are indicators of employee well-being; they are also identified as drivers for change" (p. 130). The authors also indicate that there is a strong connection between the social status and work performance, as low levels of well-being are likely to be linked to absenteeism. They are likely to have implications for the health conditions of employees, as absenteeism is reported to relate to stress, depression, or anxiety, or occupational ill health in general (Collins and Perry 2015, p. 135). The financial cost of such occurrences in the working place is high enough to emphasize the importance of the issue for the economic and social sectors of a selected nation.

One major consequence that research of the area has had over years is questioning the stereotypes that have been associated with African American job performance. This effect was described by Minchin (1999), who addressed the issue diachronically showing how racist views affected the perception of the African American employees' work productivity. According to the author, a 1969 article revealing the high rates of work effectiveness registered among African American workers in textile industry was perceived by a wide number of managers with skepticism. Among them was Robert Gardiner, the personnel manager of the company Dan River Mills, who confessed in a letter to his colleague that this news contradicts all reports of African Americans' work productivity. His sources claimed that such employees "are shiftless, lazy, don't want to work, and leave as fast as they are hired" (Minchin 1999, p. 265). White employees of Dan River Mills claimed the rates of absenteeism are considerably higher among African American employees and explained this by their laziness. Many line managers tended to adopt this view based on their own observations (Minchin 1999, p. 265).

However, Gardiner was determined to find out which of the two opposing views is correct and undertook a profound analysis of the employee performance in the company. The results showed that "blacks had lower turnover and absenteeism rates than whites and slightly higher productivity" (Minchin 1999, p. 265). Another finding concerning absenteeism was that the common view of the African American workers as having trouble with maintaining the discipline necessary for industrial jobs was not accurate (Minchin 1999, p. 266). Though it was hard for the investigators to believe that the actual data was so different from the commonly adopted attitude, they had to agree that racial issues distorted the actual performance rates.

There is a strong connection between the job performance of men and the rates of father absenteeism in African American families, which is also linked to the history of discrimination in the American society. As Threlfall and Kohl (2015) stressed, "institutionalized racism caused minority men to be marginalized, first from the labor market, and then from the family. Governmental policy must acknowledge the link between father absence and job absence" (p. 15). Whereas Threlfall and Kohl claimed that financially successful men are likelier to enter a marriage and assume responsibility for their children, Hudson et al. (2012) indicated that for many African American families, the issue of employment and the ability to provide for children is an issue of ultimate importance. Hudson et al. (2012) also emphasized that "the influence of biased perspectives in social sciences and human service professions has reinforced the perception of African American men as absentee fathers without acknowledging their historical socio-economic circumstances" (p. 114). What appears extremely relevant is that maintenance of a permanent employment has always served as a hurdle to the fulfillment of the fathering role for African Americans, as an emphasis on the provider role presupposed maximum effort invested in job performance (Hudson et al. 2017, p. 114). There is a difference between an African American father who is absent because he chooses this option and the one who cannot be involved in child care because of unemployment or incarceration. In the traditional mode of a family, which is also applicable to the African American community, manhood depends largely on the ability of men to provide for and sustain their families (Hudson et al. 2012, p. 116). Therefore, the functions of providing and caring for children seem to be in conflict in a wide range of cases. If the father is unable to provide his family with a comfortable living and maintain permanent employment, the adverse effects of the situation on the family might include "decision-making patterns, equilibrium, and hence, the family's inability to navigate a hostile environment" (Hudson et al. 2012, p. 116).

Absenteeism of African American adult male parents in the family sphere is of great importance, as in this case the social well-being comes to dominate the relationships of each individual family, impacting the social fabric profoundly. The above-mentioned arguments imply that there is a strong connection between the cultural, social, and economic spheres of life, which seems to indicate that the dysfunctional trends in the African American family are likely to affect job performance and the overall patterns of people's relations within a society.

According to Threlfall and Kohl (2015), "as society has progressed into a more technologically advanced social, economic, and academic age, the multiple uncertainties and social ills surrounding the family unit have come into focus" (p. 784). At the same time, this interest is conditioned by not only the intention to find out what is wrong but also taking steps to eliminate the existing issues. Researchers and therapists tend to pay special attention to the African American family unit, as the dysfunctions that seem to haunt it seem to be directly linked to the deplorable economic conditions that a growing number of such families have to face. According to Collin and Perry (2015), the problem of the father absenteeism in African American families is regarded by researchers as causing a wide range of social issues and irritations, among them increasing rates of black male juvenile crime and consequently, a growing number of African American juveniles with criminal records. Other problems include growing tendencies in the number of illegitimate children and children that are parented by single mothers and growing reliance of African American female-headed families on the state (Collins and Perry 2015, p. 784).

Earlier, Austin (1978) indicated that the pathological consequences that broken homes entail are likely to have more adverse effects on African American children than white ones. Since girls are more emotionally vulnerable, absence of a father might inflict a serious trauma on them. This results in the crime statistics that showed a trend for African American girls from broken homes to be more inclined to become involved in public policy offences, among them sexual offences, running away, and ungovernability. However, boys from broken homes seem to be more inclined to become juvenile delinquents, both in terms of personal and property offences (Austin 1978, pp. 487–488). Therefore, the issue of parent absenteeism has been quite relevant for a considerable time. Recent studies have shown that the problem has not lost its acuteness over years.

The situation has a profound effect on the children's economic and mental well-being first. Thames et al. (2003) compared the harm that is caused to African American children by father absenteeism and being raised by unwed mothers with the traumatic experience of being educated within a system of racially segregated schools: "The evidence of harm is as strong as or stronger than the evidence gathered [...] to justify the massive civil rights mobilizations of the last century" (Thames et al. 2013, p. 154). Thames et al. (2013) stressed that raising a child is fraught with challenges for African American families in the US even in the most favorable circumstances. However, the situation is substantially aggravated for most children from such families due to the family structure and economic considerations.

On average, children from single-parent families seem to be in a disadvantageous position in comparison with those who have two parents. According to Collins and Perry (2015), "a growing body of research, carefully controlled for a wide variety of variables, including race, income, housing location, and other factors is showing that father absence, in and of itself, is a major cause of negative outcomes in children's lives" (2003, p. 155). The proportion of children living in poverty is five times higher for those who are brought up in single-parent families than those who have two parents. Also, father absenteeism is closely connected with children absenteeism from school, as children from a family without a father are twice as likely to drop out of high school. Their academic performance can also be affected. Moreover, statistics shows young males raised in single-parent families are twice as likely, and those brought up in stepfamilies are thrice as likely to fall into crime and commit offences that are punishable by imprisonment terms. Finally, such children are at risk of becoming victims of crime, or child abuse (Collins and Perry 2015, p. 155).

Threlfall and Kohl (2015) concentrated on the social, interpersonal, and economic issues that are directly evoked by father absenteeism and have to be faced by single mothers from the African American communities. The researcher considered social support from friends and family that can become both a coping aid and an aggravating circumstance. Such support from friends and family tends to affect parenting by way of reflecting on the maternal psychological well-being. If this support is positive, it is likely to lessen the strain of parenting responsibilities, especially in single-parent families where the burden of responsibility is carried by one person instead of two. In such families, friends and extended family members are directly concerned in the support and care of children, which is extremely important in the case of low-income single African American mothers. One should mind, however, that the relationships with friends and family might as well not be positive but conflictual, which results in greater depressive symptoms and parent stress (Hudson et al. 2012, p. 366). Jackson explained that "social support buffers stress associated with economic hardships or child temperament" (Hudson et al. 2012, p. 366). Another interesting finding was elicited by Collins and Perry from a comparison of married mothers with and without parenting support from their husbands with single mothers (Hudson et al. 2012, p. 366). It appeared that married mothers who had not sufficient support from their husbands were the least adequate parents, which was used as evidence of the crucial role of fathers' support for mothers' parenting adequacy (Hudson et al. 2012, p. 366).

The critical importance of the father is also emphasized by Thames et al. (2013) who indicated that the various adverse effects of fatherlessness include the possibility of the diminished level of cognitive competence, poor performance at school, and low self-esteem. Moreover, possible problems include promiscuous sexual activity and a higher risk of emotional problems, violence, substance abuse, or other delinquent behaviors. This is explained by the common belief that "fathers influence their children's moral development, academic achievement, and competence in social interactions and emotional and mental health" (Hudson et al. 2012, p. 14).

A recent report presented by Chiles (2013) suggests that the consequences of father absenteeism in the African American households remain unchanged: "Research reveals that black boys (and girls) raised in a household without their father's presence are at a dramatically greater risk of drug and alcohol abuse, mental illness, suicide, poor educational performance, teen pregnancy, and being ensnared in the criminal justice system" (Chiles 2013, p. 126). Mothers who have no support from their children's fathers lack parenting tools that might compensate for the missing fathers. Research into these mothers' attitudes toward their sons shows a lack of understanding and unawareness of the inescapable differences between boys' and girls' psychological patterns. More specifically, many African American boys' mothers from single-parent families tend to view their sons as "mildly retarded girls," as their developmental paces seldom coincide. This difference is compensated over time provided that boys have the necessary home environment and parenting (Chiles 2013, p. 126). This is another point why father absence is extremely harmful for boys' development because the father's image adds perspective to the development of a boy's behavior. Moreover, the aspect of self-esteem is also addressed as "a father is less likely to accept the low expectations for the boy" (Chiles 2013, p. 127).

The socialization patterns of boys are affected by the fact that mothers anticipate the hardships that their sons will have to face in future, being part of the African American community. Wishing to boost toughness in them, which they believe will help them withstand difficulties of life, they often limit their demonstrations of love and affection. From their viewpoint, excessive manifestations of maternal love are likely to make their sons overly soft. However, as Chiles indicates, "the unfortunate result is that the boys wind up lacking the love and affection they desperately need" (Chiles 2013, p. 127). Violent antisocial behavior might be caused by the boys' attempts to show their "manliness."

The economic implications of African American adult male absenteeism as an issue in family relationships are suggested by Latunde and Clark-Louque (2016), who claimed that societal institutions that are inherent in the classical perception of the family are to a degree responsible for the weakness of the father-child bond and absenteeism of fathers. According to the author, "maintaining the sacred status of the mother-child dyad continues the myth of separate, i.e. gendered, spheres of life. The cultural assumption of separate spheres links public/work/masculine and private/family/feminine" (2016, p. 15). Men are unwilling to concentrate on family issues for fear of being regarded as showing a lack of commitment to their jobs, or non-masculine.

The social effects of the situation that has been described are far-reaching. The immediate consequences (dysfunctional trends in the family patterns and development of violent and anti-social behavior in children) are exacerbated by their cyclic nature. Collins and Perry (2015) mentioned that the proportion of illegitimate children in African American families, which used to be mainly a problem characteristic of low-income households and reached the rate of approximately 25 percent, in 2005 reached the proportion of two thirds and climbed up the socioeconomic scale (para. 7). Those who regard family as a major American value speak of the decline of marriage and traditional family, seeing deplorable consequences that this development might have in future.

Collins and Perry (2015) mentions two probable explanations to the current situation. On one hand, in the low-income households such developments as unemployment, early death of African American adult males, and disproportionate incarceration make these males unavailable for marriage or family relationships. At the level of higher incomes, African American women are likelier than men to graduate from school and college and earn the credentials that make them desirable for marriage (Collis and Perry 2015, para. 8). As a result, one may assume, fathers are not part of a family; without their stabilizing influence, children risk experiencing various economic (financial difficulty), social (delinquent behaviors and socialization hardships), and cultural (a distorted image of masculinity) issues described above. Taken as a general trend, all these issues have a nationwide importance, affecting not only one social group but exerting influence on the US society and culture in general via interpersonal and business relations.

Addressing the Problem of Male Absenteeism in African American Families

As it was mentioned before, the goals of this book include not only an insight into the basis, peculiarities, and effects of African American adult male absenteeism in families. But the experiences of the individuals, organizations, and entire social spheres that made attempts to ameliorate the situation to suggest an efficient method to improve the situation is also an important element of the book. Since the range of associated problems, as Abrams et al. (2017) mentioned, is quite wide; there are various planes on which the issue might be handled.

First, as Richardson and Van Brakle (2013) stressed, it is important to acknowledge the complexity of the African American family as a domain influenced by a variety of factors—historical, economic, and social. It is a system that interacts with other systems, and understanding its structure and functions requires utilization of a historical perspective. The African American family structure, as a result, should be regarded as "an adaptation to a set of sociopolitical conditions existing in the family's wider social and ecological environment" (Richardson et al. 2013, p. 212).

Richardson and Van Brakle (2013) stressed the importance of family therapy in order to address the issue of instability in families where fathers provide no or insufficient child care. There are varying techniques whose utilization might be of assistance. For example, Minchin's "joining techniques" that were described in 1974 might be considered as generally sensitive to the peculiarities of the African American family structure. However, some elements of these techniques, such as escalating stress, emphasis on the symptom, and boosting emotional intensity in order to manipulate the mood might meet with lack of understanding from some African American families. These methods are quite radical and might be perceived as attempts to undermine integrity, authority, and respect within the families. Therefore, these techniques may be used exclusively after the establishment of a trusting relationship (Richardson and Van Brakle 2013, p. 252).

Collins and Perry (2015) recommended another, ethnohistorical, approach in family therapy as more efficient. Within the framework of this approach, "a meticulous, detailed narrative account of each person's (unique) emotional experience of the many race-related stress and historical traumas could complement existing intergenerational approaches that focus primarily on intra- and interfamilial issues and events" (Collins and Perry 2015, p. 252). Families may use this approach to construct their own narrative that is likely to counteract negative sociocultural metanarratives and build up more liberating narratives indicating the beginning of the healing process. Thus, family therapy may be of assistance in the process of reinforcing the fraying social fabric of the family institution in African American communities at the level of individual households' needs.

Barton et al. (2015) indicated, however, that males tend to be less responsive to treatment than females. Even if they agree to receive therapy in order to improve the relations within a family and are willing to give more care to their children, "African American men bring with them much […] suspicion […], in addition to a feeling of defensiveness about how the therapist may judge them in the fathering role" (Barton et al. 2015, p. 77). They might also be reluctant to confide in therapists because they associate the latter with mainstream organizations they do not trust. Therapists should, therefore, pay special attention to signs of ambivalence and react to them with due flexibility and creativity. As a result, even limited signs of an increase in parental involvement may entail individual as well as structural changes in a family (Barton et al. 2015, p. 78).

The last decade of the twentieth century witnessed a variety of nation-scale steps toward understanding and defining fatherhood for noncustodial parents and their children. In 1995, President Clinton established an initiative fostering positive father involvement with the noncustodial children. The work of federal agencies to reduce parental neglect of children, increasing trends in the number of single-mother families and father absenteeism was grounded in research that indicated a direct connection between parental involvement and children's well-being (Barton et al. 2015, pp. 211–212). The initiatives undertaken by federal agencies were meant to do the following: to increase self-sufficiency rates of families by way of improving child support collection, creating additional employment opportunities for low-income men, as well as cooperating with the private sector initiative referred to as Partners for Fragile Families; also to provide necessary assistance to help parents share the emotional, financial, and legal responsibilities associated with fatherhood; to reinforce the parent-child bonds through focusing on paternity establishment and providing block grants to state initiatives in order to encourage noncustodial parents to enter access and visitation programs; to foster fathers' involvement in the early developmental years of their children, to take preventative measures against premature fatherhood via dissemination of information on reproductive health initiatives among male youth and fostering family planning services for males (Stanik et al. 2013, p. 212).

The implementation of these initiatives faced several issues, among them lack of staff and technological support, as well as multifaceted and overwhelming needs of the target population. In the African American communities, the clientele rates were quite low. However, there was a strategic drawback in all these initiatives. Abrams et al. (2017) mentioned that the social policies aimed at meeting the requirements for economic, emotional, and social well-being of children from the African American communities have been mostly ineffective. Despite the recognition of the problem and various strategies to improve the situation, black children continue to suffer from higher rates of poverty, teenage pregnancy, school dropouts, and various health conditions associated with the low standard of living and substance abuse. Social policies mentioned above, as viewed by Hamer, cannot be called comprehensive. They only attempted to address the issue by forced establishment of children's paternity, pursuing live-away fathers to impose formal paying the child support on them and modifying the welfare policy (Barton et al. 2015, p. 211).

The welfare strategies initiated by President Clinton were taken over by the Bush administration given its strong social agenda, drawing on conservatism and the alarming rates of childbirth outside marriage. The modification to the previously pursued policy consisted in shifting the focus from promoting parental involvement as such to the encouragement of "healthy marriages." Thus, Bush's initiative highlighted the role of healthy relationships within a couple to promote stability and reduce the rates of breakup and divorce, and not unconnectedly, non-marital births (Abrams et al. 2017, p. 522). However, there were studies suggesting that it is not the institution of marriage per se but the quality and pattern of the residential relationship within a household that influences the child's development most. As Abrams et al. (2017) mentioned, "in a longitudinal book of low-income families, unwed fathers who were prenatally involved during the pregnancy were more likely to be involved with their partners and children at age three because they had transitioned into a more committed relationship" (Abrams et al. 2017, p. 524). This book implied that in low-income households where absence of stability, permanent employment, and low educational attainment may be extremely acute issues; promoting marriage alone might not result in the desired benefits for children and families (Abrams et al. 2017, p. 524). This observation is extremely relevant for this book, given high rates of poverty in families with absentee fathers. Critics of the Healthy Marriage promotion initiative charge that its limitations are conditioned by its one-size-fits-all nature, which is inescapably linked to certain failures (Abrams et al. 2017, p. 525). Stanik et al. (2013) mentioned a specific program, the Concordia Project, that sought to address the issue of absentee parenthood among African American fathers. The basis for the program was created in 1996 and was entitled "The University of Hard Knocks and Higher Learning." Young fathers participating in the program expressed the wish to develop social confidence through gaining various social experiences. They wanted to get a school graduation certificate, attend theater or a concert to face the "other" world themselves and have an opportunity to show it to their children. As Jones put it, "they wanted to experience mainstream American opportunities without losing their connection to home and community. It was important for them to do those activities and still "remain black"" (Stanik et al. 2013, p. 250).

Working with enthusiastic African American fathers was based on a new comprehensive paradigm. The University provided opportunities for low-income, non-custodial male parents aged sixteen to twenty-eight. The overall goal was essentially to help men prepare for the positive engagement in the children's lives and develop respect for their mother regardless of their attitude toward the latter. The program implied case management, employment, transportation, other support services, as well as peer and parenting groups. There was no funding allocated to aid men outside the indicated age limits, but the project would include any fathers who sought ways to improve their parenting patterns (Stanik et al. 2013, p. 250).

The program developed over time, involving more innovative projects. The new development was named the Concordia Project and used the previously described program as a basis. The project harnessed the allied effort of the Saint Paul Urban League and the National Practitioner Network for Fathers and Families (NPNFF) to train family practitioners instilling the importance of fathers' involvement in the family affairs. The project gives opportunities to fatherhood practitioners wishing to facilitate the involvement of parents in their children's lives by way of assisting them in enrolling in universities and colleges and earning a degree (Stanik et al. 2013, pp. 253–254). The achievements of the initiative suggest that training professionals having the skills and knowledge to address the issue of father absenteeism in African American families might be a powerful tool, especially if these professionals are African Americans who experienced the problem firsthand.

Unlike many researchers who concentrate on the emotional and mental condition of women and children in African American families, Collins and Perry (2015) studied the mental conditions of fathers. It appears that economic and social hardships often result in high depression and stress rates. The major implication of the book, as seen by Richardson and Van Brakle (2013), is that the problem of mental health issues of African American fathers is essential and should not be neglected (p. 295). One might assume that with due attention paid to the needs of fathers as well the level of stability and emotional comfort within a family the father-child bond might become stronger.

Speaking about the effectiveness of addressing the issue of absent fathers in African American communities, Richardson and Van Brakle (2013) mentioned models for successful social programs that operate several common components. First, they do not limit their emphasis to teenage fathers, as difficulties are experienced by men in varying age groups. There is also a focus on fathers as nurturers and caregivers, as participants should feel comfortable when caring for their children and expressing their affection (Richardson and Van Brakle 2013, p. 265). The programs should directly address the value sets of men to help them develop an understanding of parental care actions as "the most masculine activities in which any man can engage" (Richardson and Van Brakle 2013, p. 265). Also, there is a clear focus on education, which is believed to liberate the mind and eliminate a wide range of limitations that a lack of education imposes on people. It is important to keep in mind though that education implies not only formal degree but the knowledge and breadth of outlook. As Richardson and Van Brakle (2013) noted, "education (learning to problem solve and think) allows one to critically analyze and reflect upon situations confronting us and to develop survival strategies that can permit us to thrive" (Richardson and Van Brakle 2013, p. 266). In terms of education, an awareness of oneself is followed by an awareness of oneself being part of an environment (Richardson and Van Brakle 2013, p. 266).

Another principle distinguishing successful programs is the inclusion of the children's mothers (Richardson and Van Brakle 2013, p. 266). Parents' development of respect and appreciation of each other's activities is likely to be more successful if these activities are shared by them. Finally, vocational activities should be included into every male involvement program because "it is important that men accept responsibility for helping to rear their children and to aid in the financial provision of their families" (Richardson and Van Brakle 2013, p. 266). Men should learn to search for jobs, maintain their employment, and develop professionally. Program participants should also be provided with the necessary mental intervention due to high rates of exposure to stress and depressive conditions (Richardson and Van Brakle 2013, p. 266).

Chapter 4

Adult African American Males— From Their Perspective

Letters with informational flyers were sent to family members explaining the nature of the research. They were asked to identify applicable fathers for the book and discuss the possibility of participation in the research with them. If the father is interested, he was asked to contact the researcher for further information. These fathers were asked about other fathers who were interested in this research by the family members or researcher as well. These fathers followed the same procedure and contacted the researcher if they are interested. This was designed to avoid any confidentiality concerns.

The African American adult males' descriptions of their experiences were analyzed for commonalities and shared experiences. From these commonalities and shared experiences, themes and categories of meaning were developed and reported in the findings. Convenience sampling was used in this book due to the access and availability of the population.

Twenty-six interviews were conducted and a total of fourteen questions were asked during the interviews. From these questions several themes emerged from seven of the questions as follows: (1) views on marriage (the interviewee's opinion on the institution of marriage); (2) as a child (interviewee) whether or not they grew up and living in a two-parent home (the interviewee's experience growing up in a two parent home or the lived experience of not growing up in a two parent home); (3) feelings about female head of households (the interviewee's view on females managing a household without a male partner); (4) the ability to change present circumstances as they relate to their children (the interviewee's thoughts on how they could make their lives different or better if they could change their relationship with the mother of their child(ren); (5) relationship with their children (do the interviewees have a relationship with their children); (6) relationship with their father (7) employment, is it a factor?

Views on Marriage

Throughout the interviews twenty-two males saw marriage as a wonderful union between two people that love and respect each other. They believe the marriage holds the key to some measure of success in life and provides levels of stability, safety, and protection for the children. They saw love as an important ingredient which should be nurtured regularly.

Two interviews saw marriage as a foundation for real relationships apart from raising a family. These views placed strong emphasis on the marriage but less on whether the children played a part in the overall family structure. The belief is that if the marriage is strong, the family (if any) was strong as well. Interestingly, having children was not the core theme.

One interview viewed marriage as an important purpose of raising children, while another interview did not want to be married. The interview revealed that the individual had seen several marriages end in separations and divorces. The results of these separations created disruptive environments for the children and according to the interviewee and led to truancy and maladaptive behavior in the children that included disrespect for authority.

One interview viewed marriage as an institution whose time has gone by. The interviewee did not like the idea of marriage and enjoyed being "free of bondage." The idea of marriage did not appeal to him because of the challenges he observed in other relationships.

He saw females as domineering and controlling, constantly making demands upon males and creating great strain on the relationship.

Overall, African American adult males embraced the idea of the institution of marriage. The interview revealed that most had an appreciation for the value of marriage, in most cases borne from cultural lens of their upbringing, which is associated with having seen a few more male heads of households during their lifetimes. The interviews revealed that African American adult males have very solid favorable views on marriage. Many concur that, if their circumstances were different, they would have married the mother of their children and assumed their roles as head of household.

Growing Up in a Two-Parent Home or Not

Twenty-six interviews were conducted resulting in thirteen individuals stating they grew up in a two-parent household with a mother and father throughout the duration of their childhood. The interviews reveal that having parents in the home was important, but more importantly whether the father in the home was an individual that mentored the children and was available to them when needed. Out of this population, nine individuals report that they had a good healthy relationship with their parents and with their fathers. The fathers provided guidance, attended important events in their lives, and encouraged them to be successful in life both academically and personally. Four of the interviews point out that a two-parent home has its pros and cons. Four interviewees report they did not communicate with their fathers on a regular basis, with others reporting they often do not get along with their fathers at all. Interviewees report that some fathers were overly strict, absent on some occasions due to work requirements, or was an alcoholic.

The balance of the interviews resulted in thirteen individuals reporting that they grew up in a single-parent household. Of this population, three had an average to above average relationship with their father. He would visit from time to time and attempted to be a part of their lives. These relationships established foundation for open communication over the years. Two interviews reveal that the individual was raised by a grandparent, whereas neither the biological mother or father had an active role in child rearing. During a couple of interviews, three individuals reported that their father was incarcerated. In these cases, the father was at home for a short period of time during the interviewee's childhood, but their father's incarceration lasted beyond their youth years at home and spanned well into their young adult years. These individuals report not having or wanting a relationship with the father, and by their accounts, the fathers did not want a relationship with their sons. One interview revealed that one father had no interest in the interviewee and had another family. This father did provide some means of child support but did not actively pursue a relationship with the interviewee. Some reports reveal that the fathers left the home when the interview was very young (under the age of 10 years). One case was due to divorce and one other departed and never returned. In each of these cases the fathers did not participate in the life of the interviewee. Only in one interview did the individual report not ever meeting his father. His mother told him who he was, but a face to face meeting did not take place.

Female Head of Household

The interviews provided information of the views of African American adult males regarding female head of households. Twenty-six interviews were conducted which asked the question "How do you feel about female heads of households and why? Ten individuals interviewed were very understanding to the challenges associated with being in charge and managing a household. The interviewees believe that if a woman is running a household, it could be by chance or choice. Some of the interviewees experience this situation first hand. They had a mother or grandmother who managed the affairs of the home. The men discussed some of the challenges such as maintaining enough finances to pay bills, providing enough food to eat for the family, and or maintaining the upkeep of the residence. Often these females did not have male companionship but did get some assistance from time to time from their maternal father, brother, uncle, or grandfather.

Several of the interviews revealed a strong disdain for the men who left the women behind resulting in the women becoming a head of household. Sixteen interviews placed emphasis on "the failure of men." In the interviews, many were angry because, according to them, when the male decided to leave the home and was never an active member of the family, the stress associated with a one-parent home often created turmoil and chaos. Children would often cry, during their childhood stage (ages two to four), without a clear antecedent. The children manifested abandonment concerns which would be displayed as disrespect for adults which included, verbal and some occasions physical aggression toward others, truancy, elopement, and suicidal ideation. Due to the male's failure to take care of the family, the interviewees believe that another generation of children would grew up thinking that absentee fathers are the norm. It was clear that their frustration over the situation of female head of households was very personal, creating levels of frustration, particularly if it was their mother who was forced into this capacity.

The Ability to Change Present Circumstances as they Relate to their Children

Twenty-six interviews were conducted resulting in several individuals concluding they made major mistakes in not staying with their families and marrying the mothers. Seven individuals blamed their poor choices on immaturity. These individuals were afraid of responsibility, lacked courage, and possessed levels of selfishness which indicated they were only interested in the act of sex while not considering the short-term consequences (sexually transmitted diseases) or the long-term consequences (pregnancy, child rearing). These subjects knowingly or unknowingly believed that if pregnancy occurred, it was the mother's responsibility. Interestingly, during these interviews none of the subjects denied being the father of the child(ren). This group, however, indicated they would not have married the mother of their child(ren). Three individuals did not take responsibility for their actions but blamed the use and failure of condoms as the reason for the pregnancy. They never wanted children and are angry that the condom failed. This anger appears to be misplaced such as in the failure to blame themselves.

The balance of the interviews revealed a group of men who are more family centric. Thirteen individuals' views of marriage and family have similarities to the group in this section, but they had a desire for marriage. As discussed, if this thirteen of men could change things, they would marry the mother of their child(ren), help raise the family, improve their education level thereby getting better jobs and not spend their time "chasing" women. This group saw marriage modeled either within the confines of their parent's home or within the home of an extended family or the family of close friends. This group indicate they are or want to be an active part of the life of their children and conclude that if they could undo what has occurred, they would. This group appear to be good fathers to their children.

Relationship with their Children

The twenty-six interviews revealed various levels relationships. These men, depending on whether they have a desire to build and maintain a relationship with their children, identified how often they visit their children and the types of interactions they have with them. The number of visits, in most cases, is a good indication whether the relationship with their children is a strong and healthy one or whether more work is needed to improve the relationship.

Themes were gathered from the interviews conducted regarding the type of relationship the men had with their children and the frequency in which they visited them. The outcomes of these themes are: solid relationship—weekly visits; average relationship—monthly visits; below average relationship—quarterly visits; poor relationship—brief visits over the years

Men in general, want to have good relationships with their children. A strong contributor to whether the relationship is strong between the father and the children is dependent on the relationship between the biological father and biological mother. When the mother is positive toward the father or when she uses positive words regarding the father, the relationship between the father and children proves to be more stable. The reverse is true when the mother is very negative toward the father or uses negative words regarding the father, the relationship with the children trend toward poor outcomes. During the interviews, nine interviews indicate they have solid relationship with their children. These men spend time with their children in person and or on the phone weekly. These men participated in school activities and were engaged with their children by taking them out to eat a meal, went to movies, church, went shopping, played sports, and did other activities appropriate to the age of the child.

The next group of ten men were less actively involved with their children but maintain good relationships with them. Their visits were less frequent, generally about once a month. Their participation with their children was very similar to the above group. The frequency of the visits was tied to their proximity to the children as impacted by the father living in a different town or county or work schedules.

The next group of four men had a below average relationship with their children due to the infrequency of the visits. These men generally had other family relationships but had a desire to remain in the lives of their child. When available, they would telephone call their children and visit quarterly. The activities in which they participated in are like the other groups discussed above.

This final three individuals have poor relationships with their children. It was revealed that the father did not have good communication with the mother due to a fundamental difference in parenting styles as well as their unresolved past relationship issues. These men had very little contact with the child sometimes going several months without seeing them or talking to them. The men indicate when they do see the children, the children's response to them is that of seeing a distant relative or perhaps meeting a stranger for the first time.

Relationship with Your Father

The interviews presented some emotional moments for some of the subjects regarding relationship with their fathers. Discussions regarding fathers sparked emotions of resentment, anger, loneliness, sadness, abandonment concerns, fondness and hatred. Fifteen interviews had a good or average relationship with their father. These men presented with bright affects and responded with words such as mentor, good friend, good father, role model, supporter, encourager, educator, confidant, hard worker, provider, and leader. The balance of the interviews presented men who did not have a good relationship with their father. Eleven interviews presented with flat, irritable and blunted affects and responded with words such as "no good," "never saw him," "saw him on occasion," "he was a drunk," "didn't care about me," "cared about his other children," "never there for me," "bad role model," "I know where he lives but I will not visit him," "never knew him," "I don't have a relationship with him." This group of men had the greatest concern for their futures and the futures of their children in the context that they may have some of the same mannerisms and personality just like their biological father. Admittedly, they report they are failing in relationships to some degree with their own children. This group appear to be more isolated, lacking solid male relationships thus void of positive male role models.

Employment

Employment can make a difference in effective parenting, relationships with a spouse and children, or impact one's self-esteem. For this book, employment, from the perspective of the African American adult male's absentee rate among families is somewhat mixed. During the interviews, the breakdown of the impact of education was categorized (Appendix E).

Conclusions 1

What are the self-reported reasons that African American adult males give for the disproportionate decline in male-led households from their perspective?

African American adult males report that the decline in male-led households is borne from the apathy associated with youth, pressure associated with getting married and remaining married, and the lack or desire to parent children. Many report that after the female partner becomes pregnant, they develop a fear of responsibility and want to remain "free" of the responsibility to raise children. In many cases, the children are born out of wedlock and to young mothers. These males did not plan nor did they have any intention of parenting children. Education, incarceration, and careers goals or achievements rate very low as to the reason for the decline. Divorce plays a role but not to the degree that it impacts the overall census.

Conclusions 2

How do African American adult males' beliefs regarding fatherhood and parenting influence their interaction with their children?

Their responses to this question were often met with enthusiasm and a bright affect. In many cases, fatherhood is reflective of how these males saw fatherhood modeled during their childhood. Positive modeling provided a template for any future and long-lasting results. Even if the father did not remain in the home, he would, based on the interviews, be a good father, spending quality time with the children as often as he could, be depending on work schedules, life style, or other relationships (marriage to someone other than the mother of his children) or the availability of the children based on their mother's schedule. The relationship that father had with his parents provided a strong foundation for emotional bonding with the children. These fathers worked hard toward ensuring their children received the father's attention. As explained in the interviews, the fathers ensured that the children received the guidance, medical attention (as needed), and funds necessary to provide a healthy and happy life. These men did not shy away from their responsibilities as fathers and parenting by integrating their lives into the lives of their children. Many report spending weekends, holidays, and summer vacations with their children. Others would attend sporting events, recitals, and other school or community activities with their children.

Conclusions 3

What are the explanations for African American adult males abdicating their roles as head of household? (African American males not being the head of the household in its traditional definition).

Throughout the interviews, it was clear that twenty two individuals saw marriage as a wonderful union between two people that love and respect each other. However, many report that the fear of responsibility plays a large part as to why these males are not living with the mother of their children as well as whether they can cohabitate with the biological mother of their children. Many discussed the immaturity of the male at the time of the pregnancy, the fear and pressure of having to support a female partner and children, the lack or absence of good employment, and the challenges associated with having to deal with the biological mother's family such as her parents and siblings.

In every case, all report that the pregnancy was unintentional and that they were not ready for it. They cite that they wanted to continue to "enjoy" life before they became "tied down." Many did not consider the possibility of becoming fathers prior to their participation in sexual relationships with the mother, and in many cases, pregnancy did not occur immediately. This gave them a false sense of security thereby leading to unanticipated parenthood. Often, because of poor modeling by their fathers and mothers, some males saw the parenting as the responsibility of the mother, while the male provided shelter, clothing, and food. Additionally, because of poor modeling, these males did not have the desire to lead a household but felt more secure just taking care of themselves. They all admit that this is a selfish attitude and know that this attitude can be impactful and long lasting both in their lives and the lives of their children.

References

Abrams, J. A., Maxwell, M. L., and Belgrave, F. Z. 2017. "Circumstances beyond their control: Black women's perceptions of Black manhood." *Sex Roles, 1*(12). doi: 10.1007/s11199-017-0870-8.

Adkison-Johnson, C., Terpstra, J., Burgos, J., and Payne, E. D. 2016. African American child discipline: Differences between Mothers and Fathers. *Family Court Review, 54*(2), 203-220. doi: 10.1111/fcre.12214.

Armah, T. 2015. "The next Black America: Obstacles amidst opportunities for Black families." *American Journal of Orthopsychiatry, 85*(5), S55.

Austin, R. L. 1978. Race, father-absence, and female delinquency. *Criminology, 15*(4), 487–504.

Baker, C. E. 2014. "African American fathers' depression and stress as predictors of father involvement during early childhood." *Journal of Black Psychology, 40*(4), 311. doi:10.1177/0095798413486480.

Barton, A. W., Kogan, S. M., Cho, J., and Brown, G. L. 2015. "Father involvement and young, rural African American men's engagement in substance misuse and multiple sexual partnerships. "*American Journal of Community Psychology 56*(4), 241–251.

Bellamy, J. L., Thullen, M., and Hans, S. 2015. "Effect of low income unmarried fathers' presence at birth on involvement." *Journal of Marriage and Family, 77*(3), 647–661.

Bianchi, S. M., Casper, L. M., and King, R. B. 2005. *Work, family, health, and well-being.* Mahwah, NJ: Lawrence Erlbaum Associates, Inc., Publishers.

BMWK staff. 2013. "The importance of fatherhood, From A to Z." Retrieved from http://www.Blackandmarriedwithkids.com/2013/04/the-importance-of-fatherhood-from-a-to-z/

Research perspectives. *Developmental Psychology, 22*(6), 723–742.

Brown, J. 2012. *Growing yourself up: How to bring your best to all of life's relationships, (3–5).* Wollombi, NSW: Exisle Publishing.

Bryant, K., Haynes, T., Greer-Williams, N., and Hartwig, M. 2014. "Too blessed to be stressed": A rural faith community's views of African-American males and depression. *Journal of Religion and Health, 53*(3), 796–808. doi: 10.1007/s10943-012-9672-z.

Bush, L. and Bush, E.C. 2013. "Introducing African American male theory." *Journal of African American males in Education, 4*, 6–12.

Chiles, N. June 2013. "Saving our Sons: The war within. Special Report." *Ebony,* 126–129.

Collins, W. L. and Perry, A. R. 2015. "Black men's perspectives on the role of the Black church in healthy relationship promotion and family stability." *Social Work and Christianity, 42*(4), 430–448.

Costa-Ramalho, S., Marques-Pintoa, A., and Ribeiro, M. T. 2017. "The retrospective experience of climate in the family of origin and dyadic coping in couple relationships: pathways to dyadic adjustment." *Journal of Family Studies, 23*(3), 371–388.

Donnellan, H. and Jack, G. 2009. *The Survival Guide for Newly Qualified Child and Family Social Workers: Hitting the Ground Running.* London, UK: Jessica Kingsley Publishers.

Doyle, O., Pecukonis, E. V., and Lindsey, M. A. 2015. "Correlates and consequences of father nurturance in an African American College Sample." *Journal of Family Issues, 36*(7), 880. doi: 10.1177/0192513X13501665.

Fathers' Rights. 2013. *Father absence in America: turning the tide on fatherlessness.* Retrieved from http://dadsrights.com/index.php/father-absence-in-america-turning-the-tide-on-fatherlessness.

Franks, A. D. 2010. *African American fathers and absenteeism*. In M. Shally-Jensen (Ed.), Encyclopedia of contemporary American social issues (pp. 782–791). Santa Barbara, CA: ABC-CLIO.

Greene, R. R. 2011. *Human behavior theory and social work practice*. New Brunswick, NJ: Transaction Publishers.

Heckman, J. J. 2011. *The American family in Black and white: A post-racial strategy for improving skills to promote equality*. NBER Working Paper No. w16841. Retrieved: https://ssrn.com/abstract=1776777

Holzer, H. J., Offner, P., and Sorensen, E. 2005. "Declining employment among young Black less-educated men: The role of incarceration and child support." *Journal of Policy Analysis and Management, 24*(2), 329–350. doi:10.1002/pam.20092/abstract.

Hudson, D. L., Neighbors, H. W., Geronimus, A. T., and Jackson, J. S. 2012. "The relationship between socioeconomic position and depression among a U.S. nationally representative sample of African Americans." *Social Psychiatry and Psychiatric Epidemiology, 47*(3), 373–81. doi: 10.1007/s00127-011 0348 x.

Kogan, S. M., Lei, M., Grange, C. R. Simons, R. L., Brody, G. H., Gibbons, F. X.,… and Chen, Y. 2013. "The contribution of community and family contexts to African American young adults' romantic-relationship health: A prospective analysis." *Journal of Youth and Adolescence, 42*(6), 878–90. doi: 10.1007/s10964-013-9935-3.

Kogan, S. M., Yu, T., and Brown, G. L. 2016. "Romantic relationship commitment behavior among emerging adult African-American men." *Journal of Marriage and Family, 78*(4), 996–1012.

Latunde, Y. and Clark-Louque, A. 2016. "Untapped resources: Black parent engagement that contributes to learning." *The Journal of Negro Education. 85*, 72–81.

Lofquist, D., Lugaila, T., O'Connell, M., and Feliz, S. 2012. "Households and Families: 2010." Census Bureau No. C2010BR-14, U.S. Census Bureau, Washington, DC. Retrieved: http://www.census.gov/prod/cen2010/briefs/c2010br-14.pdf.

McVeigh, K. 2013. "Working mother's sole breadwinners for 40% of US families, book shows." *The Guardian.* Retrieved from http://www.guardian.co.uk/world/2013/may/29/working-mothers-breadwinners-families-pew

Meschede, T., Thomas, H., Mann, A., Stagg, A., and Shapiro, T. 2016. "Wealth mobility of families raising children in the twenty-first century." *Race and Social Problems, 8,* 77–92.

Minchin, T.J. 1999. *Hiring the Black Worker: The Racial Integration of the Southern Textile Industry, 1960-1980.* Chapel Hill, NC: The University of North Carolina Press.

Moore, N., Wright, M., Gipson, J., Jordan, G., and Harsh, M., … Murphy, A. 2016. "A survey of African American men in Chicago barbershops: Implications for the effectiveness of the barbershop model in the health promotion of African-American men." *Journal of Community Health, 41*(4), 772–779. doi: 10.1007/s10900-016-0152-3.

Non, A. L., Gravlee, C. C., Mulligan, C. J. 2012. "Education, genetic ancestry, and blood pressure in African-Americans and whites." *American Journal of Public Health, 102*(9), 1559–65. doi: 10.2105/AJPH.2011.300448.

Richardson, J. B., and Van Brakle, M. 2013. "The everyday struggle: social capital, youth violence and parenting strategies for urban, low-income Black male youth." *Race and Social Problems, 5*(4), 262–280.

Ritter, J., and Taylor, L. J. 2011. "Racial disparity in unemployment." *Review of Economics and Statistics, 93*(1), 30–42.

Robinson, D. M., and Reio, T. G.2012. "Benefits of mentoring African-American men." *Journal of Managerial Psychology, 27*(4), 406–421. doi: 10.1108/02683941211020 7.

Schumacher, D. C. 2008. The effects of fatherlessness on the behavior and academic achievement of the adolescent African American adult male. (Doctoral dissertation). Bethel University, Arden Hills.

Seaton, E. K., Neblett, E. W. Cole, D., and Prinstein, M. 2013. "Perceived discrimination and peer victimization among

African-American and Latino youth." *Journal of Youth and Adolescence, 42*(3), 342–50. doi:10.1007/s10964-012-9848-6.

Stanik, C. E., & Riina, E. and McHale, S. M. (2013). "Parent—Adolescent relationship qualities and adolescent adjustment in two-parent African American Families." *Family Relations, 62*(4), 597–608. doi: 10/1111/fare.12020.

Strong, M. E. 2012. *Church for the Fatherless: A Ministry Model for Society's Most Pressing Problem.* Downers Grove, IL: InterVarsity Press.

Taylor, R. J., Mouzon, D. M., Nguyen, A.W., and Chatters, L. M. 2016. "Reciprocal family, friendship and church support networks of African Americans: findings from the national survey of American life." *Race and Social Problems, 8*(4), 326–339.

Thames, A. D., Hinkin, C. H. Byrd, D., Bilder, R. M., Duff, K. J., ... Streiff, V. 2013. "Effects of stereotype threat, perceived discrimination, and examiner race on neuropsychological performance: Simple as Black and white?" *Journal of the International Neuropsychological Society 19*(5), 583–93. doi: 10.1017/s1355617713000076.

Threlfall, J. M. and Kohl, P. L. 2015. "Addressing child support in fatherhood programs: perspectives of fathers and service providers." *Family Relations, 64*(2), 291–304.

Timpe, Z. C. and Lunkenheimer, E. 2015. "The long-term economic benefits of natural mentoring relationships for youth." *American Journal of Community Psychology, 56*(2), 12–24.

Unger, H. G. 2007. *Encyclopedia of American education: A to E* (3rd ed.). New York City, NY: Infobase Publishing.

Varga, C. M. and Gee, C. B. 2017. "Co-parenting, relationship quality, and father involvement in African American and Latino Adolescents." *Merrill-Palmer Quarterly, 63*(2), 210-236.

Warren-Findlow, J., Seymour, R. B., Brunner, H. and Larissa R. 2012. "The association between self-efficacy and hypertension self-care activities among African-American adults." *Journal of Community Health, 37*(1), 15–24. doi: 10.1007/s10900-011-9419-6.

Williams, A. D., Banerjee, M., Lozada-Smith, F., Lambouths, D., and Rowley, S. J. 2017. "Black mother's perceptions of the role of race in children's education." *Journal of Marriage and Family, 79*(4), 932–946.

Williams, T. T., Mance, G., Caldwell, C. H., and Antonucci, T. C. 2012. "The role of prenatal stress and maternal emotional support on the postpartum depressive symptoms of African American adolescent fathers." *Journal of Black Psychology, 38(4),* 455. doi: 10.1177/0095798411433842.

Appendix A

Interview Questions for Selected Participants

1. Are you aware that only 32 percent of African American households had an adult male as head of the household in 2011? Why do you think this is the case?
2. What is your level of education?
3. Are you currently employed? What is your occupation?
4. What is your view on marriage?
5. What do you see as the problem with African American families today?
6. Did you grow up in a two-parent household? If yes, describe your experience living with your father. If no, describe your experience living without your father.
7. Describe your childhood experiences as they relate to African American adult males.
8. How do you feel about female heads of households and why?
9. Why are you not living with your children now?
10. Is it difficult to live in a separate dwelling than that of your children? Why or why not?
11. If you could change your present circumstance as they relate to your children, what would you do differently?

12. Describe your relationship with your children.
13. Is your father alive? What is your relationship with your father?
14. How would the African American community benefit from this book?

This questionnaire/survey was formulated based in part on a dissertation by James Gore (Printed). Gore, James Renard. Seattle University, ProQuest, UMI Dissertations Publishing, 2001.

Appendix B

Employment

Twenty-six individuals were interviewed for this book. Below is the breakdown of their reported current employment:

- Professional (6)
  1-assistant manager—rental property
  1-auto dealership
  1-US government
  1-teacher
  1-School Social worker
  1-college administrator

- Retail (7)
  1-Best Buy
  1-Office Depot
  1-AT&T wireless
  1-Sam's Club
  1-Telecommunications
  1-Walmart
  1-SafeWay

- Military (2)
  2-Army Sergeant

- Self-employed (2)
  1-Truck driver
  1-Lawn service business

- Food service (3)
  1-McDonalds
  1-Cracker Barrel
  1-Boston Market

- Direct care (1)
  1-Group home worker

- County (2)
  1-Community center
  1-Case manager

- Contractor (2)
  1-Building contractor
  1-Construction company

- Unemployed (1)
  1-between jobs

About the Author

This is the first book in a series by Dr. Jim H. Copeland Jr. designed to highlight the opinions of African American males who currently do not hold the position of head of households. Dr. Copeland is behavioral psychologist with over fifteen years of counseling and therapy experience. The origins of his counseling experience began while serving in the military as a commanding officer, years before he earned his doctor of psychology degree. During his military career, Dr. Copeland experienced firsthand the challenges men face when navigating major relationship issues. During one incident during a tour of duty in Europe, Dr. Copeland was instrumental in saving the life of a soldier who attempted to commit suicide (by cutting his wrist) because of overwhelming marital issues.

Throughout the years, Dr. Copeland's expertise has been coveted by many of those who seek mature and relevant counseling suitable to their specific needs. He is a hands-on therapist who does not rely on just traditional book strategies but uses real life circumstances as a basis for practical application. His active strategies focus on the collaborative efforts of all family members, with emphasis placed on teamwork and mutual respect.

Additionally, Dr. Copeland works with adults with special needs, at risk youth, and special needs children. He has a passion for families and has counseled men to be leaders in their households despite social pressures.

CPSIA information can be obtained
at www.ICGtesting.com
Printed in the USA
LVHW050307280920
667274LV00001B/371